BALLOON HATS

& ACCESSORIES

**Includes free balloon pump,
30 balloons, and instructions for
making 20 different creations!**

AARON HSU-FLANDERS

CB

CONTEMPORARY
BOOKS

CHICAGO · NEW YORK

Library of Congress Cataloging-in-Publication Data

Hsu-Flanders, Aaron.
    Balloon hats & accessories / Aaron Hsu-Flanders.
      p.   cm.
    ISBN 0-8092-4383-0 : $10.95
    1. Balloon sculpture.   2. Hats.   I. Title.   II. Title: Balloon
hats and accessories.
TT926.H783   1989
745.594—dc19   89-550
                                                   CIP

Published by Contemporary Books, Inc.
180 North Michigan Avenue, Chicago, Illinois 60601
Manufactured in the United States of America
International Standard Book Number: 0-8092-4383-0

Published simultaneously in Canada by Beaverbooks, Ltd.
195 Allstate Parkway, Valleywood Business Park
Markham, Ontario L3R 4T8 Canada

For Lillian

CONTENTS

ACKNOWLEDGMENTS

This book would not have been possible without the assistance, at different points over the last thirty years, of: Dr. Ivan Ciric, David Caras, Nancy Wagner, Alan Lewitz, David Ormonde Thomas, Richard Argosh, Joshua Flanders, Roger Herzog, Ronald Wallace, Barry Mirkin, and Steve Ascheim.

Special thanks go to: Stacy Prince and Deborah Brody, my editors; Harvey Plotnick, my publisher; Cathy Mahar, my agent; and everyone at Contemporary Books, with whom it has been a joy to deal.

David Caras and Joe Skutas are entitled to free balloons for life.

The balloon-hat models, who help the book come to life, are: Vance Gilbert, Joanna Bolalek, Greta Bradlee, Johanna Franzel, Melina Franzel, Benjamin Gardner, Lillian Hsu-Flanders, Per Hagman, Chris Rozé, Chloe Wagner Caras, Mia Wagner Caras, Phokion Karas, Gail Margolis, Alan Lewitz, and David Ormonde Thomas.

CAUTION:

Although I have seen other professional performers occasionally use their mouths to form little bubbles on the tail ends of balloons, *do not* put inflated, tied balloons in *your* mouth. Balloons pop all the time, and if this should happen while the balloon is in your mouth, bits of rubber could get caught in your throat. I *never* put inflated, tied balloons in my mouth.

Also, I do not recommend letting children under the age of three handle these balloons, as these children are very likely to put the balloons in their mouths. Adult supervision is advised for all children under the age of seven.

INTRODUCTION

The phenomenal appeal of balloon hats was apparent to me long before I traveled around the country promoting my first book, *Balloon Animals*, since I had for years delighted children and adults throughout New England with large balloon sculptures that could be worn on their heads. People always loved the balloon hats the most. As soon as someone has a balloon hat on his or her head, he or she is immediately transformed!

During my promotional tour, I was able to introduce balloon hats to large audiences all across the country. The results were astounding! People of all kinds, shapes, sizes, and ages turned into trolls, elves, sorceresses, explorers, jesters, and superheroes and superheroines the minute they had a balloon hat on their heads. Some people found a certain elegance in the graceful curves and colors of the balloon hats, while others found an uninhibited playfulness in the shapes and sizes.

These simple balloons, when manipulated the right way, can spread an incredible amount of genuine pleasure and pure fun. Even people who don't quite "look" as if they'd enjoy having balloon hats on their heads go absolutely wild when they finally get one. I hope that everyone who buys this book will experience the pure joy of becoming "something else," even if just for a moment.

BEFORE YOU START

ABOUT THE BOOK

The balloon hats included in this book are creations of mine that have, over the years, proven themselves to be popular, as well as a great deal of fun. The names that I have given the hats are intended to be playful. Some of them look more like what they are named than others. Feel free to rename any of the hats if you come up with a better idea. If you come up with a really good one, please let me know; you can write to me in care of my publisher. Remember, if you wear any of these hats in a slightly different position, they become entirely new hats!

Several of the balloon hats that are presented in series are intended to be enjoyed at each of the three stages: with one balloon, with a second balloon added, and with all three of the balloons. The same is true with the four-balloon costume. All of the one-balloon hats, as well as the one-balloon belt, are quite fun all by themselves, and you shouldn't rush through the one- and two-balloon stages just to get to the final three- or four-balloon creation. Try each of the hats on in different positions and in different moods before you move on to the next one!

Please note that the hats are not presented in any order of difficulty. I would suggest beginning the series hats with the helmet, however, as certain technical information is discussed in depth in the first series. This will also help you become familiar with the language of balloons. Information on how to inflate and tie balloons appears in the beginning of the book and should be of help if you're not used to handling this type of balloon. Also, be sure you read all of the instructions for each hat before you make the first twist. It's good to know what to expect with each hat before you start.

Once you've practiced all of the hats in this book and feel comfortable creating my balloon hats and accessories, I encourage you to try inventing some of your own. The possibilities are endless! Some of the best balloon hats and accessories that I've seen were one-of-a-kind creations that first-time balloon sculptors just made up on the spot.

This book comes with a starter kit of pencil balloons, but don't be alarmed if you're not an expert by the time these balloons run out. Eventually you'll want to have a supply of balloons around all the time for those irrepressible urges that only a balloon hat will satisfy. I suggest trying to find them in your local novelty, magic, or joke shop. The balloons included in this kit are the #260 or #280 variety. If you can't find them locally or would just rather order them by mail, I've included a few mail-order sources in the back of the book.

A FEW REMARKS ABOUT THE BALLOONS

You'll want to make sure that your balloons are always reasonably fresh. To ensure this, keep them in a dry place, away from heat. Also, keep your balloons out of the direct sunlight. The sunlight makes the balloons more susceptible to popping.

You might have to file your nails down a bit if you have sharp corners on them. If you have long fingernails, you'll have to learn to twist balloons with the inside of your palm, keeping your fingernails away from the balloons. Keep your inflated balloon away from any sharp objects. If you are wearing any sharp rings on your fingers, I suggest putting them in your pocket until you are finished twisting. Don't run your hands up and down the sides of the balloon. Besides making a loud squeaking noise, this will weaken the sides of the balloon and could cause it to pop.

Remember that the balloons may vary slightly in size. Some balloons may even be a couple of inches different in length. If your balloon hat begins to look a bit different from the one in the picture, it may be because the balloon you are using is slightly longer or shorter than the one I used. Remember that your hats don't need to look exactly like the ones in the pictures. If they're a little longer, shorter, or slightly altered, they will still look fabulous.

You will usually begin twisting the balloon from the end that has the knot, toward the end that has the tail. In some cases, you will begin twisting the balloon from different points. Read the directions carefully and pay close attention to which part of the balloon I am referring to.

Smaller bubbles require a few extra twists to secure them. Whenever you make a small bubble, twist it around a few extra times to hold it in place.

You may want to give your dog or cat a balloon hat or costume. Please remember, however, that some pets like balloons and others don't. Be careful using balloons around your pet, as it may scare the animal.

One last, important point to remember is that balloons pop. This doesn't happen as often as you might think, but balloons do occasionally burst, through no fault of yours. Don't be afraid, however, to twist and pinch the balloons exactly as I have instructed, for

these balloons are made specifically for this purpose. Also, if you can't resist drawing on the balloons (and this does occasionally cause them to pop) please use a felt-tip pen.

Reminder: DON'T put inflated, tied balloons in your mouth.

INFLATING THE BALLOON

I recommend using the small hand pump included in this kit. For children or adults, these balloons are difficult to inflate with your own lungs, and the pump works quite well. Using the pump will also allow you to make as many balloon hats and accessories as you want, without getting tired from inflating them. Here are a few suggestions for inflating the balloons:

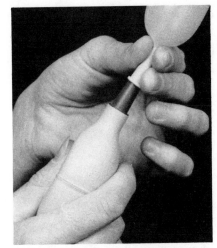

1. Stretch the balloon a few times before you inflate it. Slip the end of the balloon over the nozzle of the pump. Roll the neck of the balloon onto the nozzle about one inch. Hold it in place with the thumb and index finger of one hand. With your other hand, slowly begin inflating the balloon by squeezing and releasing the bulb of the pump.

2. Fill the balloon until there is an appropriate length of tail on the end. Each hat or accessory will require a specific amount of tail to be left at the end of the balloon when you inflate it. This tail will allow you to make many twists in the balloon. It allows the air in the balloon to expand as you make your twists.

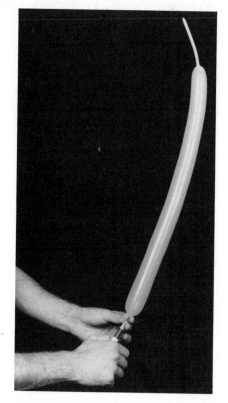

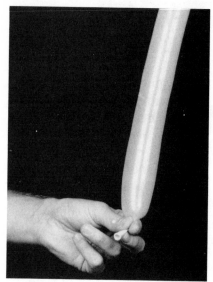

3. Slip the neck of the balloon off the nozzle of the pump, but continue pinching the neck of the balloon to keep the air inside.

TYING THE BALLOON

There are many good ways to tie a balloon. Any way that works for you is fine. These are the steps that I follow:

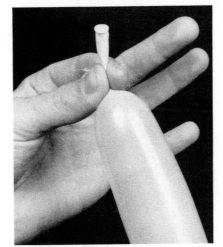

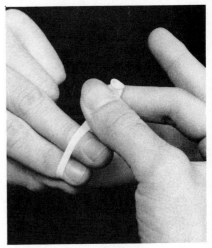

1. Let a tiny bit of air out of the balloon so that the neck of the balloon is a little longer and more flexible. Hold the neck of the balloon between your thumb and index finger.

2. Stretch the neck of the balloon over the backs of your index and middle fingers.

7

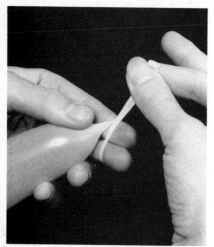

3. Continue stretching the neck of the balloon around the fronts of your index and middle fingers.

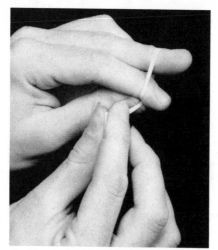

4. If you separate your index and middle fingers, you will create a small space.

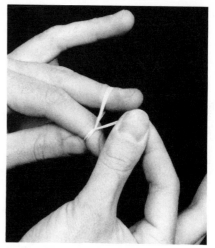

5. Push the neck of the balloon through this space.

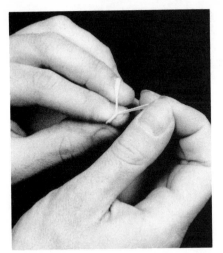 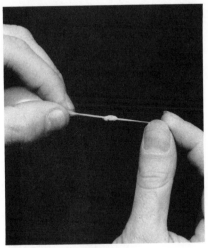 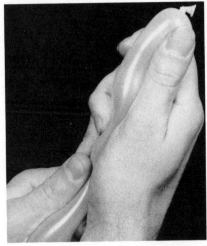

6. Holding the neck of the balloon, slide the rest of the balloon off your index and middle fingers.

7. Give a little tug, and you have your knot.

8. Before you begin twisting any of the hats or accessories in this book, squeeze each balloon gently at the knot end, to lessen the tension of the balloon behind the knot.

ONE-BALLOON AND TWO-BALLOON HATS

THE BUNNY EARS

This hat uses just one balloon and is amazingly simple to make. It is one of my favorite one-balloon creations.

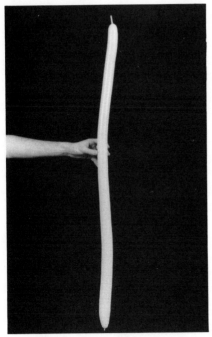

2. Wrap the balloon around the head of the person who will be wearing it, starting from under the chin and extending up to the top of the head. Point the two ends of the balloon up toward the ceiling.

1. Inflate a balloon until you have a 1-inch tail on the end, and tie a knot.

13

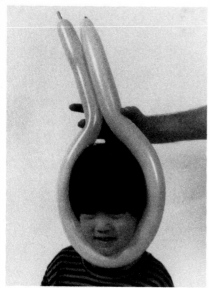

3. Make sure that the tail end and knot end of the balloon are even in height, and pinch the two lengths of balloon together at the top of the person's head.

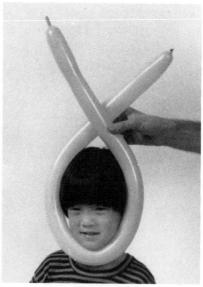

4. Twist the two lengths of balloon around each other at this point.

5. Twist them tightly, a couple of times, until they are locked together.

14

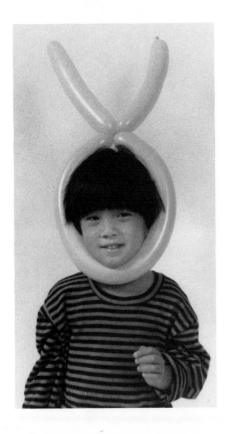

6. Straighten the two "ears" of your bunny hat, and you're ready to start hopping! This is the completed Bunny Ears.

THE RAPUNZEL

This is a stunning yet simple creation that also works as a pirate or gypsy hat.

16

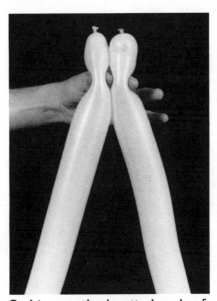

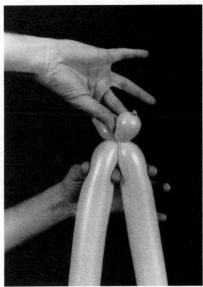

1. Inflate and knot two balloons, leaving a 1-inch tail on the end of each.

2. Line up the knotted ends of the two balloons, and with one hand pinch each of them about one inch below the knots.

3. Twist the two 1-inch bubbles that are formed by your pinch around each other a couple of times until they are locked together.

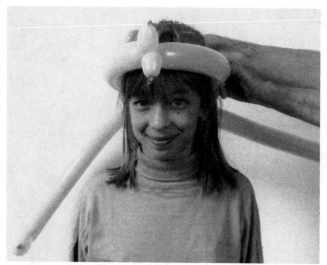

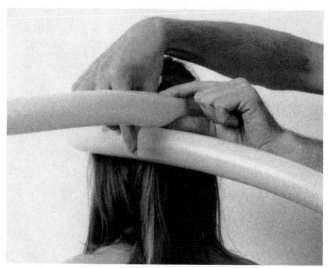

4. Wrap the two balloons around the head of the person who will be wearing the hat. Wrap them around the head from front to back, with the two 1-inch bubbles in front.

5. Cross the two balloons in back of the head, and mark with your fingers the point on each balloon where they cross.

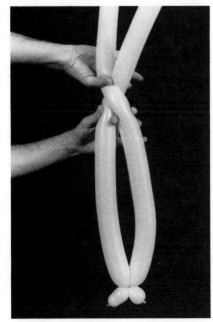

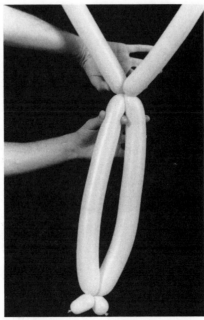

base of this hat. Throughout the book, the part of each hat that actually goes around a person's head will be referred to as the *balloon base*.

6. Take the balloons off the person's head, and twist the two balloons around each other at those points.

7. Twist them around a couple of times until they are locked together. You have just created the *balloon*

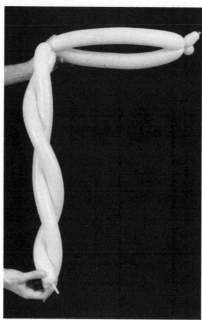

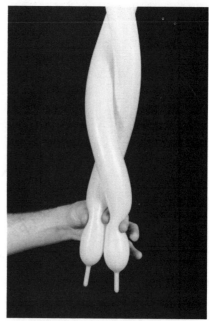

8. Take the two long sections that are sticking out from the *balloon base* and begin wrapping them around each other, like a candy cane. Start from the twist and wrap out toward the tails.

9. Continue wrapping them around each other until you get to the ends of the balloons.

10. Pinch off a small 1-inch bubble at the tail end of each balloon. Use one hand for this.

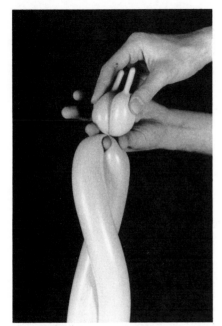

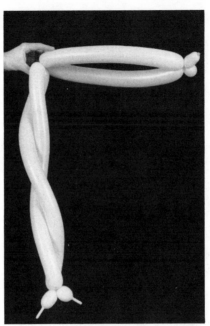

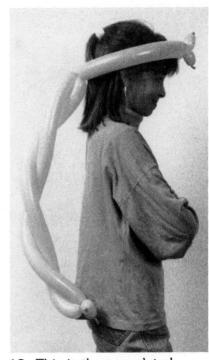

11. Twist these two 1-inch bubbles around each other until they lock together.

12. Adjust the braided section of the hat so that it points downward when the hat is on somebody's head.

13. This is the completed Rapunzel hat.

THE BUTTERFLY

This is another wonderful two-balloon hat that is made with both balloons at the same time.

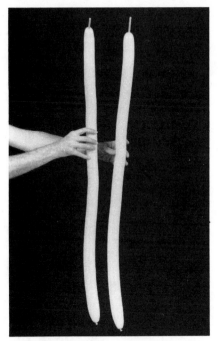

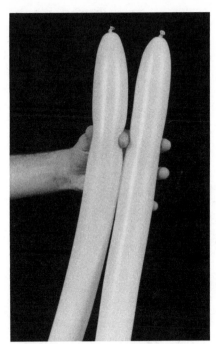

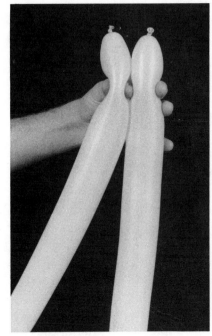

1. Inflate and knot two balloons, leaving a 2-inch tail at the end of each.

2. Line up the knot ends of both balloons.

3. With one hand, pinch both balloons about an inch below the knots.

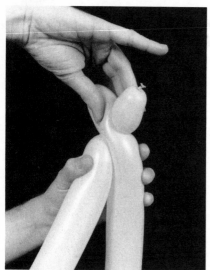

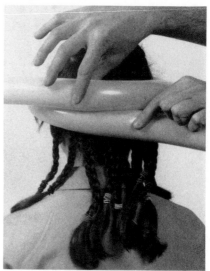

4. Twist the two 1-inch bubbles that are formed by your pinch around each other a couple of times until they are locked together.

5. Wrap the two balloons around the head of the person who will be wearing the hat. Wrap it from the front of the head around to the back, keeping the two bubbles in front.

6. Cross the two balloons in back of the person's head, and mark with your fingers the point of intersection on each balloon.

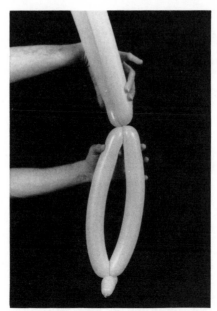

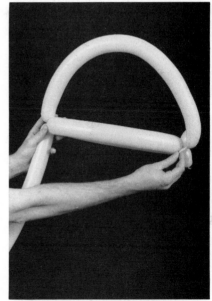

7. Take the balloon off the person's head, and twist the two balloons around each other at those points.

8. Twist them around a couple of times until they are locked together.

9. Take one of the tail ends of the balloon and bring it over in an arc to the point where your two bubbles are twisted together.

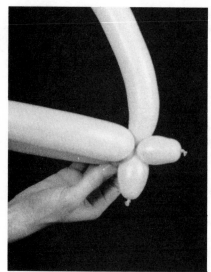

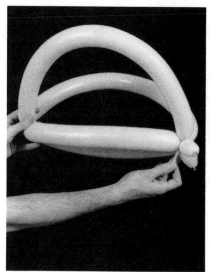

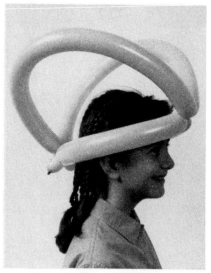

10. Wrap the tail end of the balloon around this point. Wrap it around a couple of times until it is locked into place.

11. Repeat this process with the other tail end. Bring it over in an arc to the same point, and twist it around that point a couple of times until it locks into place.

12. This is the completed Butterfly hat.

13. This hat is also fantastic
when worn upside down.
Make up your own name
for this one!

SERIES I

THE HELMET

The Helmet is a very flexible base hat that can be added to in many different ways. By itself, it is a favorite of children of all ages.

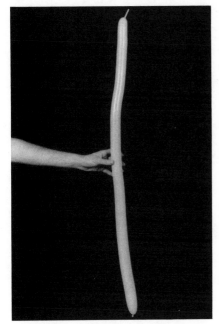 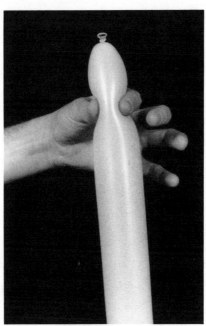 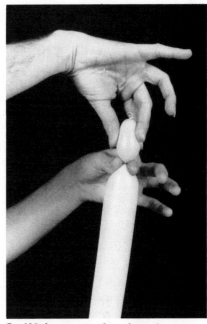

1. Inflate a balloon until you have a 1-inch tail on the end, and tie a knot.

2. Pinch the balloon one inch below the knot with the thumb and index finger of one hand.

3. With your other hand, twist the 1-inch bubble formed by your pinch around a couple of times.

31

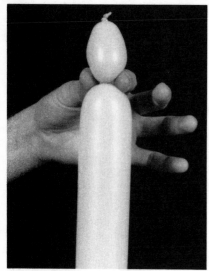

4. Hold onto this twist so that it doesn't untwist.

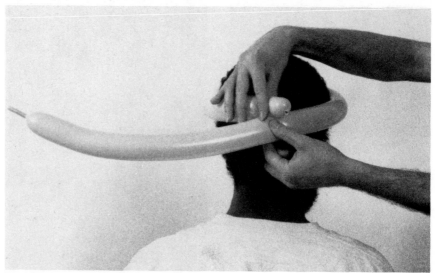

5. Measure the balloon around the head of the person who will be wearing it. With your finger, mark the point at which the twist below the 1-inch bubble meets the length of the balloon.

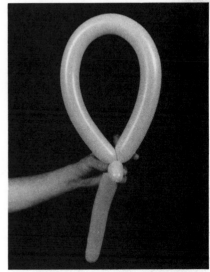

6. Remove the balloon from the person's head, and wrap the bubble around the length of balloon at the point that you've marked with your finger, to form a loop.

7. Twist the bubble around a couple of times until it is locked in place.

8. This is the balloon loop that will form the *balloon base*.

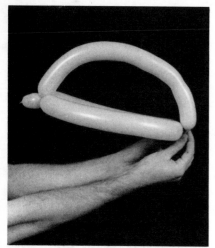 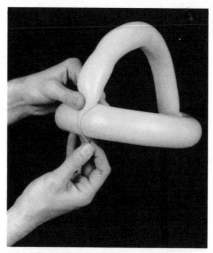 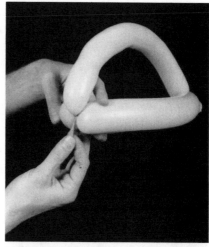

9. Take the tail end of the balloon and bend it over in an arc, so that it reaches the *balloon base* directly across from the twist.

10. Tightly wrap the tail of the balloon around the *balloon base* at this point.

11. Wrap it around a couple of times so that it will stay in place.

the bubble in back. This is the completed balloon Helmet. Try this one on a few of your friends. You'll be pleasantly surprised at their reactions.

12. Place the balloon hat back on the head of the person it was intended for, with

THE RAINBOW

This hat builds off the Helmet. It's a stunning two-balloon creation.

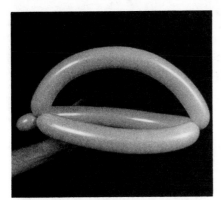

1. Begin with the Helmet, which I have just described.

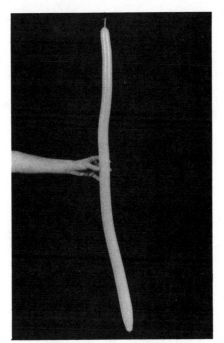

2. Inflate a second balloon until you have a 1-inch tail on the end, and tie a knot.

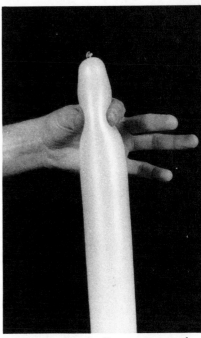

3. Pinch this balloon one inch below the knot.

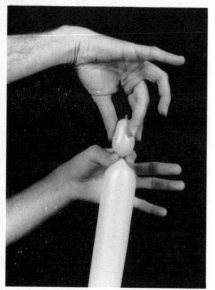

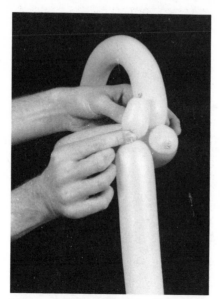

4. With your other hand, twist the 1-inch bubble formed by your pinch around a couple of times. Hold onto this twist so that it doesn't untwist.

5. Join this twist with the point on the Helmet where you twisted the Helmet's bubble.

6. Wrap the bubble of the second balloon around this same point.

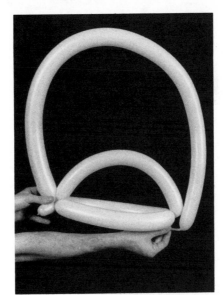

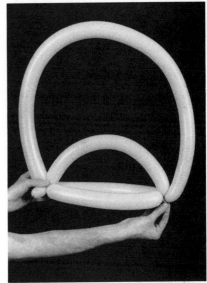

7. Wrap it around a couple of times until it stays in place.

8. Take the tail end of the second balloon and bend the second balloon over in an arc, so that it meets the point where you joined the Helmet's tail.

9. Tightly wrap the tail around this point a couple of times, so that it stays in place.

10. This is the completed balloon Rainbow hat. It's one of the most elegant two-balloon hats that I know. If you got an interesting reaction from the balloon Helmet, this one ought to cause quite a stir.

THE JESTER

This hat is an easy one, but it adds a great deal of humor and playfulness to the final creation.

41

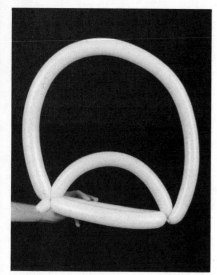

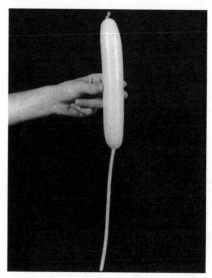

1. Begin with the Rainbow hat, which I have just described.

2. Inflate another balloon with just *six inches* of air, and tie a knot.

3. Place the midpoint of this 6-inch balloon against the top of the large balloon arc that you have just made with the second balloon.

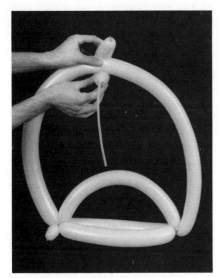 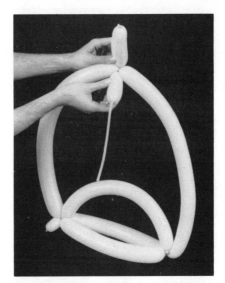 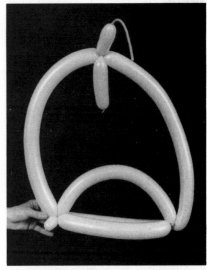

4. Tightly wrap the 6-inch balloon around the arc at this point.

5. Continue tightly wrapping the 6-inch balloon around the balloon arc for two full turns until the new balloon is locked in place.

6. Position the third balloon so that the tail end points upward when the hat is on someone's head.

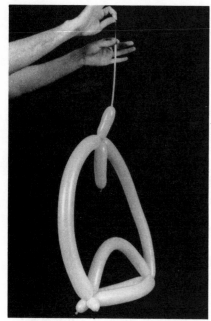

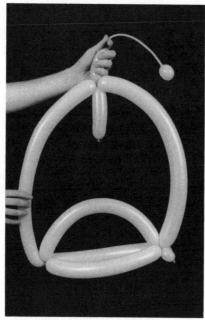

bubble pops up at the very end of the tail. It helps to fold up the long tail of the balloon while you are doing this, so that the bubble doesn't pop up in the middle of the tail.

7. Pinch the very tip of the balloon tail on the third balloon, and stretch it back and forth a few times.

8. Gently squeeze the air in the 3-inch bubble that is connected to the long tail of the balloon until a little

44

9. Let this little bubble and tail section dangle over from the top of the large arc.

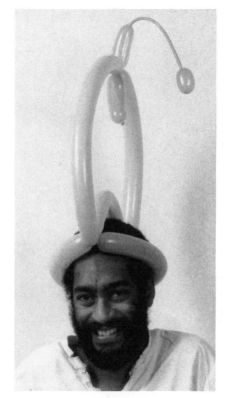

10. This is the completed balloon Jester hat. When it is worn on someone's head, the little bubble of the third balloon should dangle over the side, much like a jester's hat would have a little bell dangling from it. Enjoy being a modern-day jester. Things are somehow more humorous when you have this hat on your head. Try it—you'll see!

45

THE "I LOVE YOU" HAT

You'll find many situations and people that you'll want to make this one for. This hat is perfect as a valentine, a birthday gift, or just an adorable way to say "I love you."

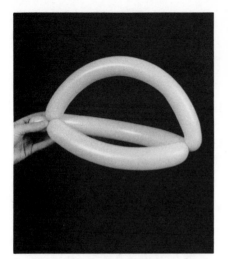

1. Begin with the Helmet, the first hat in this series.

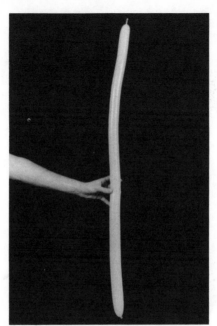

2. Inflate a second balloon, leaving a 1-inch tail at the end.

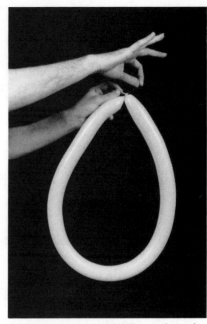

3. Tie a knot with the tail end and the knot end of the balloon to form a big balloon loop.

 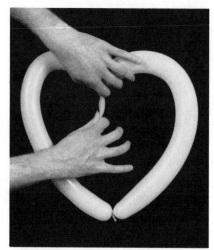 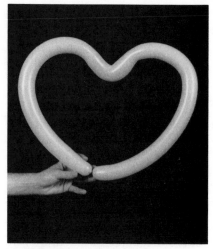

4. Double the balloon up, opposite the knot, and bring the doubled-up balloon section all the way down to the knot.

5. Gently squeeze all of the air out of the doubled-up section. Give a gentle downward tug on the part of the balloon you are squeezing.

6. When you let go, the balloon will be heart-shaped. Work with this one to perfect it; it's not that hard.

7. Return to the bottom of the heart and take hold of the knot that you have made with the tail end and knot end. Place it next to the point on the Helmet where you have wrapped the tail around the *balloon base*.

8. Grasp the tail ends of *both* balloons, and wrap them together around this point. This will lock them together and hold the heart in place on the Helmet.

9. With a little adjustment, your heart will stand up straight on the Helmet. This is a completed "I Love You" hat.

49

SERIES II

THE DAVY CROCKETT

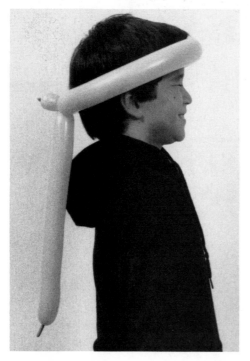

This base hat is also a very flexible one-balloon creation.

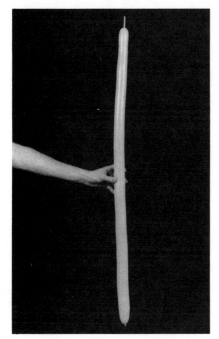

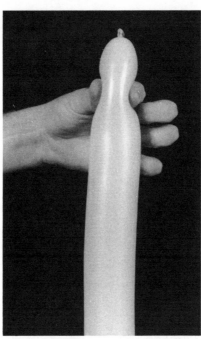

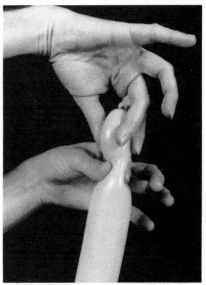

3. With your other hand, twist the 1-inch bubble formed by your pinch around a couple of times. Hold onto this twist so that it doesn't untwist.

1. Inflate a balloon until you have a 2-inch tail on the end, and tie a knot.

2. Pinch the balloon about an inch below the knot, using one hand.

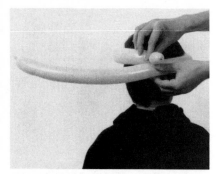

4. Wrap the balloon around the head of the person who will be wearing it, and mark with your fingers where the twist that you've made below the bubble meets the *balloon base*.

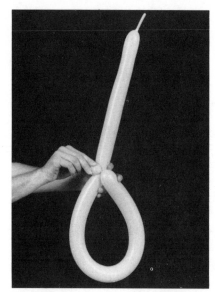

5. Take the balloon off the person's head, and wrap the bubble around the *balloon base* at the point that you were marking with your fingers.

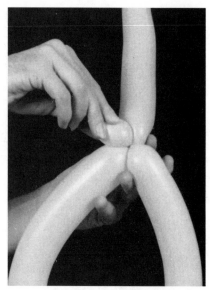

6. Wrap it around a couple of times so that it is locked in place.

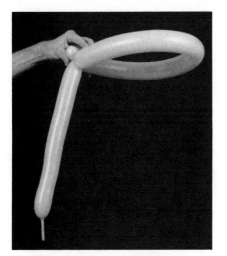

7. This will form a balloon loop that will be the base for this series. Straighten the length of balloon that lies outside the loop, and position it so that it points straight downward from the *balloon base*.

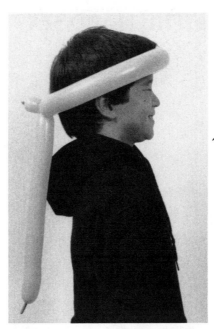

8. This is the completed Davy Crockett hat.

9. This one can also be turned upside down, so that the balloon points up and becomes the Feather hat.

THE HEADSET

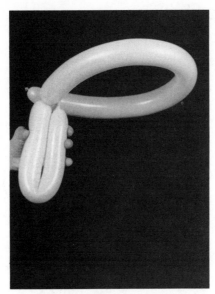

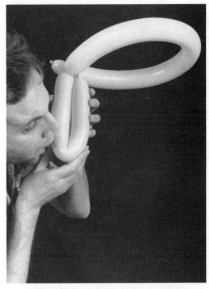

1. Begin with the Davy Crockett hat, which I have just described.

2. Take the length of balloon that lies outside the loop and fold it in half.

3. Breathe a little warm air on the balloon at the folded point.

 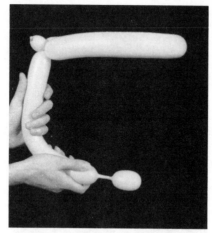

times, and squeeze the entire length of balloon away from the tail end until a little bubble pops up at the tail end.

4. Rub the balloon gently at the same point so that the length of balloon curves a little.

5. In order to make a little bubble pop up at the tail end, you will do exactly the same thing that you did in order to create the little bubble on the Jester hat. Stretch the very tip of the tail end of the balloon a few

person's mouth. This is the completed Headset, perfect for the most advanced space fantasies.

6. This little bubble will serve as the mouthpiece of the Headset. Place the hat on someone's head, with the mouthpiece pointing downward. Position it so that the mouthpiece is directly in front of that

THE EXPLORER AND THE SORCERESS

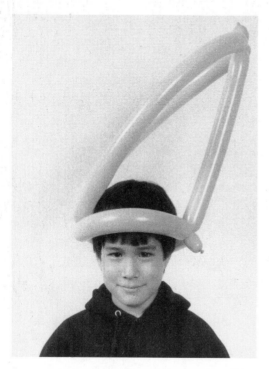

This one begins with the Davy Crockett hat, the first hat in this series. If you have already made the Headset, you can squeeze the small bubble that forms the mouthpiece back toward the twist until it disappears and straighten the section of balloon out again so that it points straight upward. You can then use this same balloon to make the Explorer.

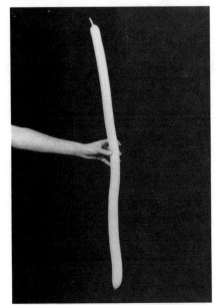

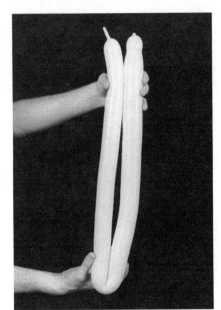

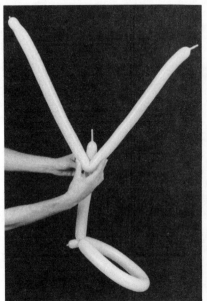

1. Inflate a second balloon until you have a 1-inch tail left on the end, and tie a knot.

2. Fold this second balloon exactly in half.

3. Place the midpoint of the second balloon against the tail end of the first balloon, about one inch from the very end.

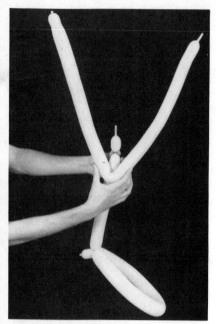 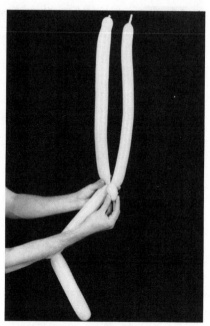 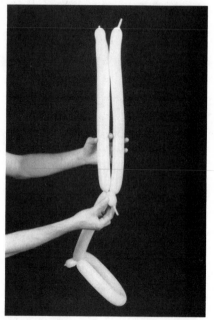

4. Make a 1-inch bubble at the *tail* end of the first balloon.

5. Wrap this bubble around the midpoint of the second balloon.

6. Tightly wrap it around a couple of times, until the two balloons are attached.

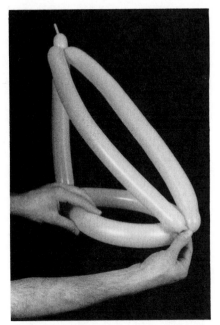

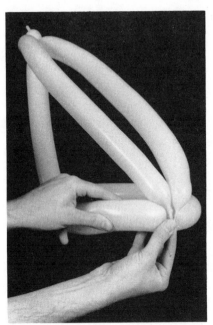

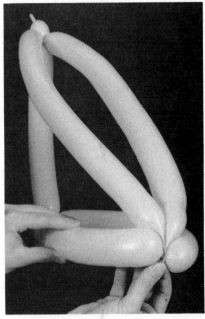

7. Grasp the knot end and tail end of the second balloon in one hand.

8. Place these two ends up against the *balloon base* opposite the twist in the *balloon base*.

9. Gently stretch both the knot end and the tail end tightly around the *balloon base* at that point.

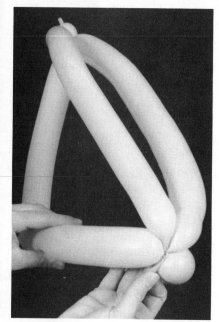

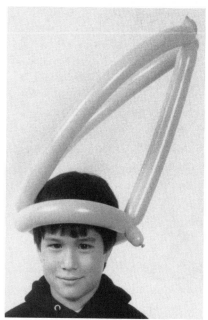

10. Stretch them around the *balloon base* a couple of times until they are locked together.

11. This is the completed Explorer hat. It can be worn sideways as the Explorer hat . . .

12. or frontways, as the Sorceress hat.

THE CROWN

This hat requires just one last addition to the Explorer hat and makes it the largest of the three-balloon hats in the book. 'Tis quite royal looking.

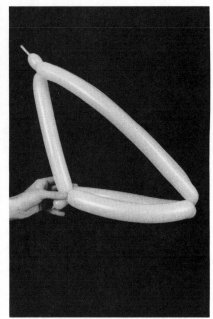

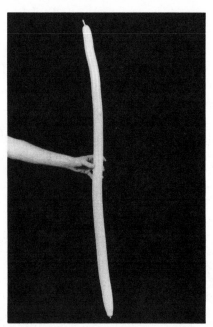

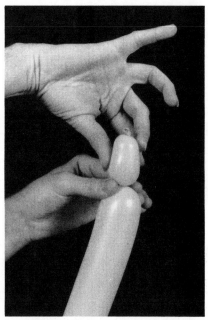

1. Begin with the Explorer, which I have just described.

2. Inflate a third balloon until you have a 1-inch tail on the end, and tie a knot.

3. Pinch off and twist a 1-inch bubble at the knot end of the third balloon.

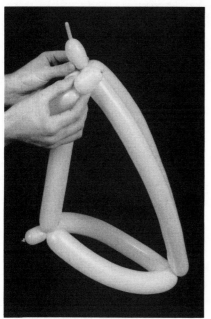

you have joined the knot end and tail end of the second balloon, forming a large arc. Place the 1-inch bubble of the third balloon next to the twisted midpoint of the second balloon.

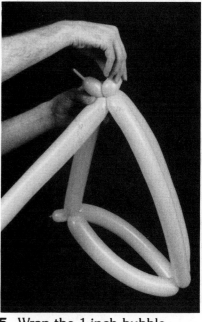

4. This entire balloon will extend from the twisted midpoint of the second balloon to the point where

5. Wrap the 1-inch bubble around the twist that already exists in the second balloon.

6. Wrap it around a couple of times until it stays in place.

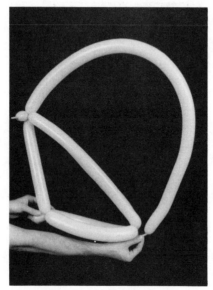

7. Take the tail end of the third balloon and place it against the twist that you have made with the knot end and tail end of the

second balloon. This will form a large arc with the third balloon.

68

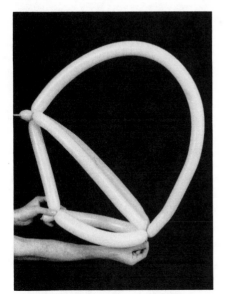

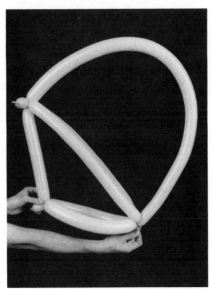

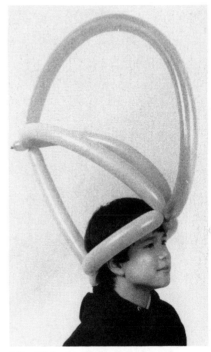

8. Wrap the tail end of the third balloon around this point.

9. Wrap it around tightly a couple of times until it is locked into place.

10. This is the completed balloon Crown.

SERIES III

THE TURBAN AND THE FLAPPER

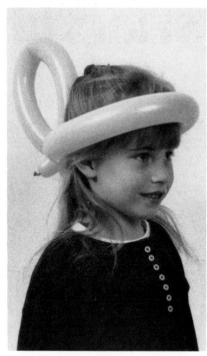

This is another one-balloon base hat that will prove quite useful to you as you begin to branch out and create some of your own balloon hats. I think that it also looks quite stunning all by itself.

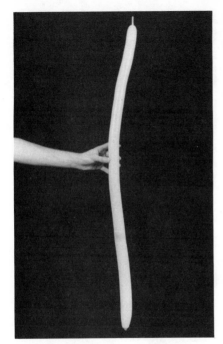

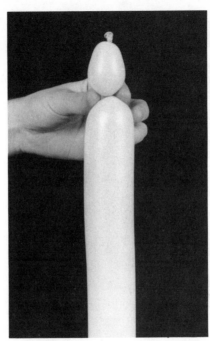

3. Measure the balloon around the head of the person who will be wearing it, and mark with your finger the point on the *balloon base* where the twist beneath the bubble meets it.

1. Inflate a balloon until you have a 1-inch tail on the end, and tie a knot.

2. Pinch off and twist a 1-inch bubble below the knot end of the balloon.

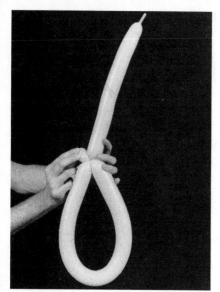 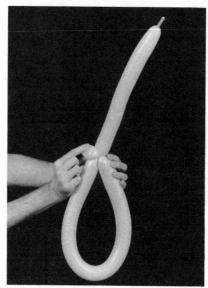 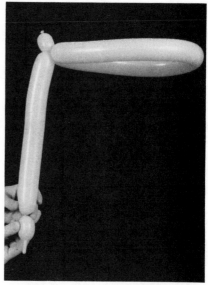

4. Take the balloon off the person's head, and wrap the bubble around the *balloon base* at the point that you've been marking with your fingers.

5. Wrap it around a couple of times until it stays in place.

6. Pinch off and twist a 1-inch bubble at the *tail* end of the balloon.

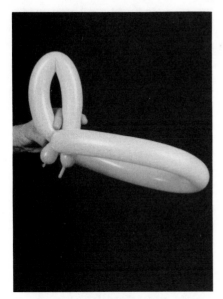 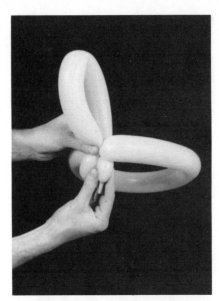 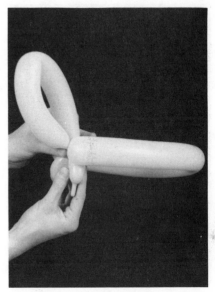

7. Fold this bubble over until it meets the point where you twisted your first bubble around the *balloon base.*

8. Gently grasp both of these bubbles with one hand, and twist them around each other a couple of times.

9. This will lock the two bubbles in place, and form a small balloon loop at one end of the *balloon base.*

10. Position the small balloon loop as shown in the photo. Also, place the two bubbles in front, one over the other.

11. This is the completed balloon Turban.

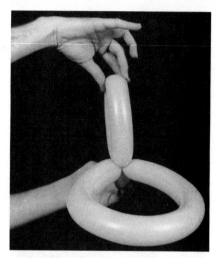

12. If you turn the small balloon loop around one-quarter turn . . .

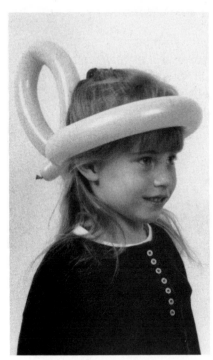

13. you have a balloon
Flapper hat.

THE HALO

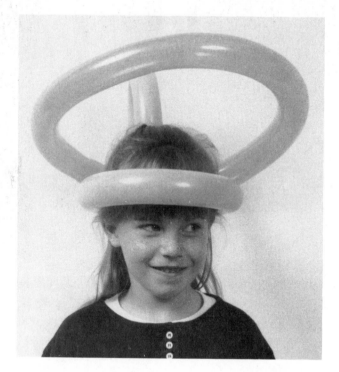

You'll be surprised at how well-behaved people become when they have this balloon hat on their heads.

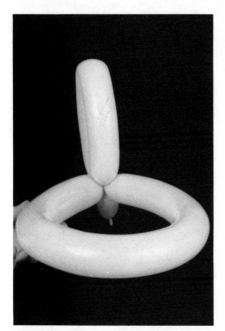

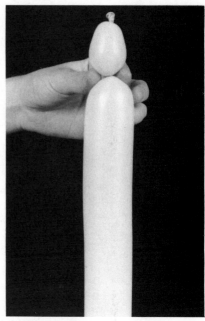

1. Begin by making the Flapper, which I have just described.

2. Inflate a second balloon until you have a 1-inch tail on the end, and tie a knot.

3. Pinch off and twist a 1-inch bubble below the knot, and hold onto it so that it doesn't untwist.

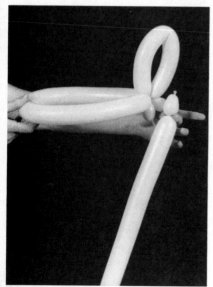

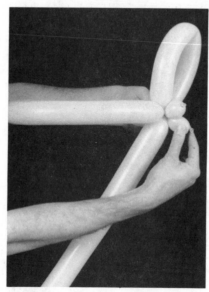

4. Wrap the bubble around the point on the Flapper where the other two bubbles are twisted together.

5. Tightly wrap it around a couple of times until the second balloon is attached to the Flapper hat at this point.

6. Bring the tail end of the second balloon around to this same point. This will form a large balloon loop with the second balloon, which will be suspended over the base of the Flapper.

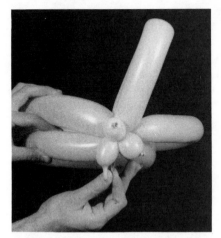

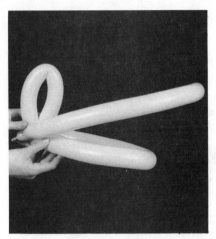

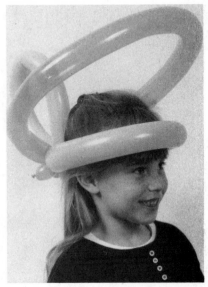

7. Wrap the tail of the second balloon around the point where all of the other twists are. Tightly wrap it around a couple of times until it stays in place.

8. Make sure that the big loop formed by the second balloon rises slightly above the *balloon base* of the Flapper. Adjust the point where all the twists meet until the second balloon rests comfortably above the *balloon base*.

9. This is the completed Halo.

81

THE TWENTY-FIRST CENTURY HAT

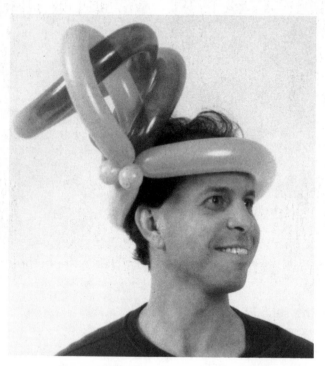

This is a wild, abstract hat that uses only two balloons. It's very, very sophisticated looking. You'll have to make a fresh balloon Flapper hat; this one doesn't build off of the Halo.

82

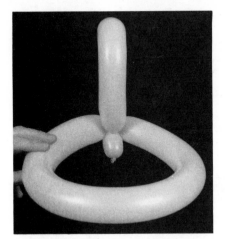

1. Begin with a new balloon Flapper hat, the first hat in this series.

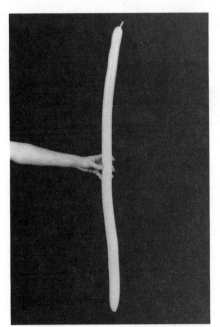

2. Inflate a second balloon until you have a 1-inch tail on the end, and tie a knot.

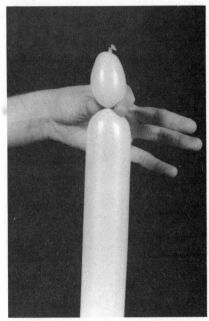

3. Pinch off and twist a 1-inch bubble below the knot, and hold onto it so that it doesn't untwist.

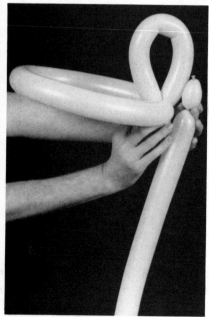

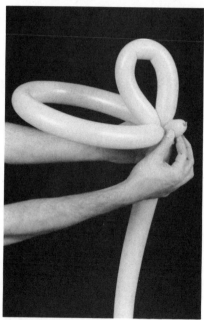

4. Wrap this bubble around the point on the *balloon base* at which you have made your other twists.

5. Wrap it around a couple of times. This will join the second balloon to the first balloon.

6. Holding the *balloon base* so the small loop is toward you and perpendicular to the *balloon base*, bring the tail end of the second balloon around in a loop so that it reaches the same spot where all your other twists have been so far. This is the same thing that you did for the Halo.

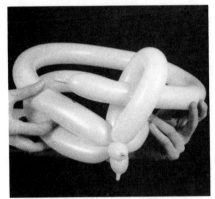  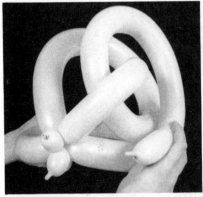

7. Instead of joining the tail end of the second balloon at this point, like you did for the Halo, pass it through the smaller balloon loop of the first balloon.

8. Continue pulling the second balloon through this loop. Pull the tail end up and over the small loop.

9. Then pull the balloon down and all the way back to the point on the *balloon base* where all of your other twists have been, as if you were going to push the second balloon through the smaller loop of the *balloon base* again.

10. Instead of pushing it through the loop, twist the tail end of the second balloon around the point where all of your other twists have been made.

11. Twist it around a couple of times until it is also locked into place at that point.

12. This is the completed Twenty-first Century hat.

THE ROLLER COASTER

This is one of the most dramatic hats I've ever made. Try wearing it in different positions on your head.

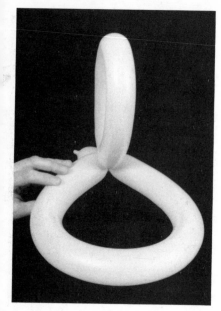

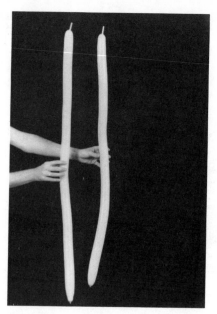

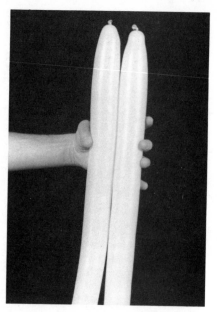

1. Begin by making the Flapper, the first hat in this series.

2. Inflate and knot two more balloons, leaving a 1-inch tail on the end of each.

3. Line up the knot ends of both of these balloons.

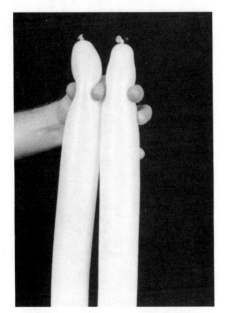

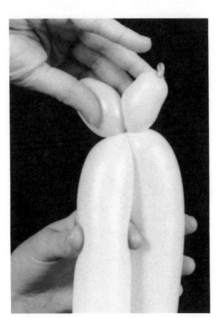

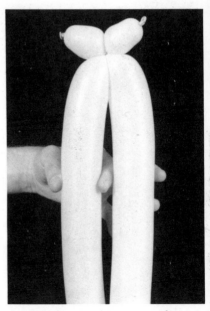

4. With one hand, pinch both of the balloons one inch below their knots.

5. With your other hand, twist the two 1-inch bubbles formed by your pinch around each other a couple of times.

6. This locks them together.

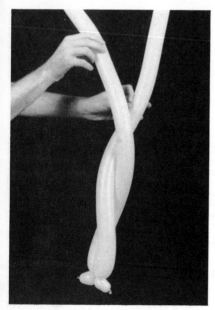

7. Starting from the twist, begin wrapping the two balloons around each other like a candy cane.

8. Continue wrapping the balloons until you reach the ends of them.

9. This is what the balloons will look like when you're this far. Unwrap them and try again if you find this a little difficult. You'll quickly get it right.

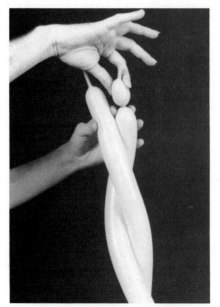 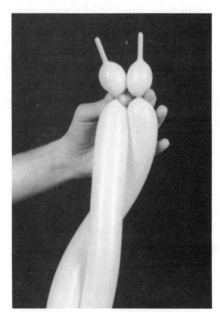 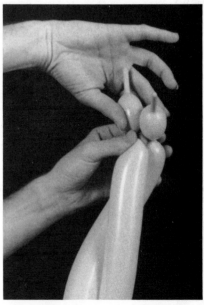

10. Make a 1-inch bubble at the *tail* end of one of the balloons, and hold onto it so that it doesn't untwist.

11. Make a 1-inch bubble on the *tail* end of the other balloon, and hold onto it also.

12. Wrap these two bubbles around each other.

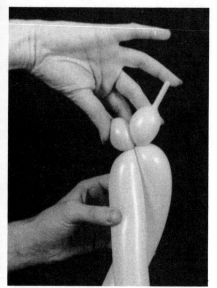

13. Wrap them around a couple of times until they are locked together.

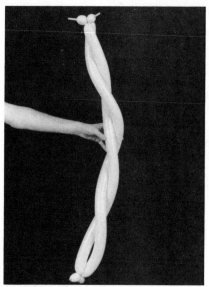

14. This is what it looks like so far.

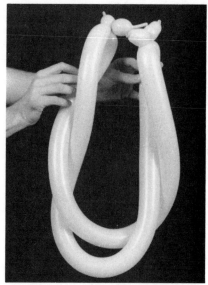

15. Bring these two bubbles together with the two bubbles at the other end, forming a big loop with the two balloons.

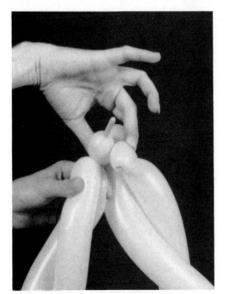

16. Join the two ends of your balloon loop by twisting all four bubbles around each other in a circle a couple of times. This locks the loop in place.

17. This is what the large two-balloon loop looks like.

18. Pick one of the four bubbles and place it next to the *balloon base* at the point where the base's twists are.

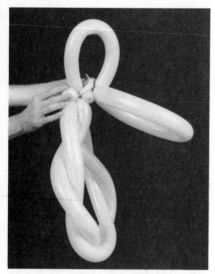

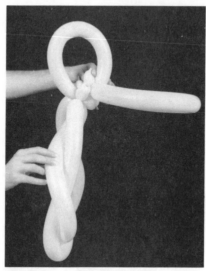

19. Wrap the bubble that you have chosen around that point on the *balloon base*.

20. You need to wrap it around only once. It will stay in place.

21. Adjust the large two-balloon loop so that it fits around the smaller loop of the *balloon base*.

22. This is the completed
Roller Coaster hat. I
suggest wearing it
sideways, so that the large
two-balloon loop points
out to the side of your
head. However, it works in
any direction, and you
should wear it the way that
you feel is just right for
the moment.

SERIES IV

THE BALLOON BELT

This one-balloon accessory can add a little extra excitement to any of the hats or can be worn by itself.

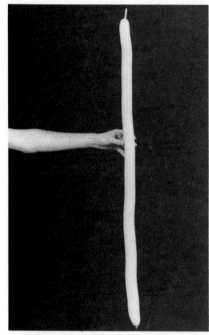

1. Inflate a balloon until you have a 1-inch tail on the end, and tie a knot.

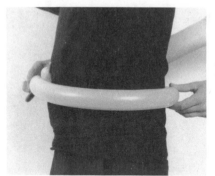

2. Wrap the balloon around your waist or the waist of the person who will be wearing it.

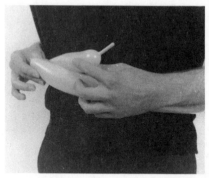

3. Cross the two ends of the balloon where they meet.

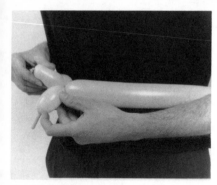

4. Twist these two ends around each other a couple of times until they lock.

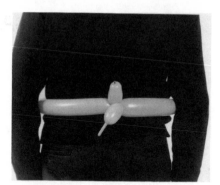

5. Position the two ends fashionably off to the side of your belt or in back if you don't want them to be visible from the front.

6. This is the completed Balloon Belt.

THE BALLOON BELT WITH A BALLOON TAIL

101

1. Begin by making the Balloon Belt, which I have just described.

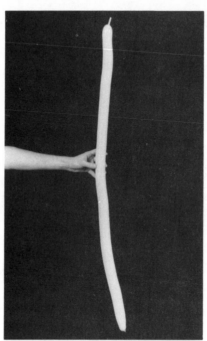

2. Inflate a second balloon until you have a 1-inch tail on the end, and tie a knot.

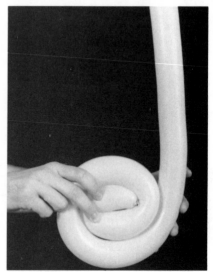

3. Starting with the end that has the knot, begin to coil your balloon. Try to go with the natural curve of the balloon.

102

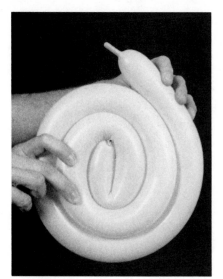

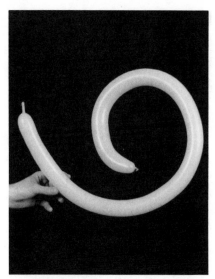

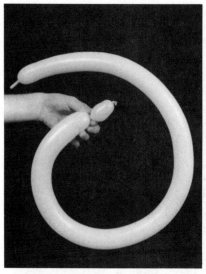

4. Continue coiling your balloon until you reach the tail end.

5. Release the coiled balloon. It should maintain a loosely coiled shape, similar to the shape of a tail on many animals.

6. Make a 1-inch bubble at the knot end of the coiled balloon, and hold onto it.

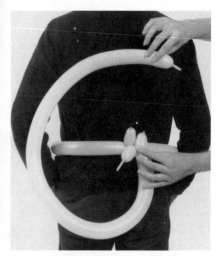

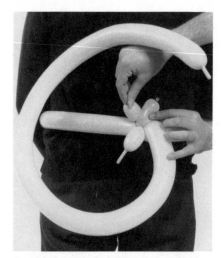

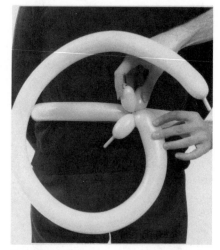

7. Place this bubble next to the Balloon Belt, at the point where the belt is knotted.

8. Wrap the bubble around the Balloon Belt at this point.

9. Wrap it around a couple of times so that it is locked into place.

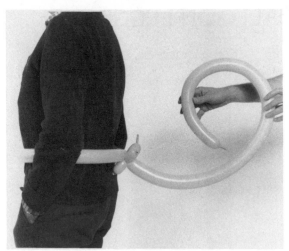

10. Position the Balloon Tail
so that the coil looks like
a long, curved tail.

11. This is the Balloon Belt
with a Balloon Tail.

105

THE BALLOON BELT WITH BALLOON LEGGING

This is another great addition to the Balloon Belt.

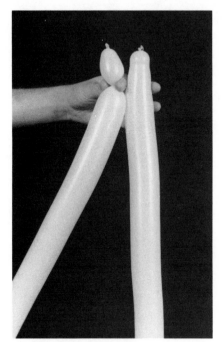

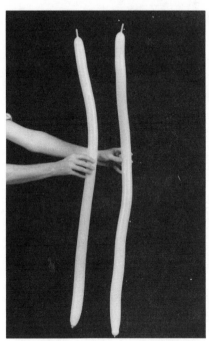

1. Begin by making the Balloon Belt, the first creation in this series.

2. Inflate and knot two more balloons, leaving 1-inch tails on the end of each.

3. Make a 1-inch bubble at the knot end of one of the balloons, and hold onto it.

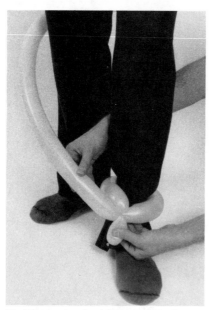

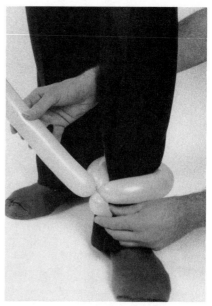

4. Wrap the balloon snugly around your ankle or the ankle of the person who will be wearing it.

5. Twist the bubble around the body of the balloon at the point of intersection.

6. Twist the bubble around a couple of times until it is locked into place.

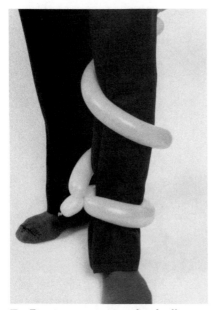
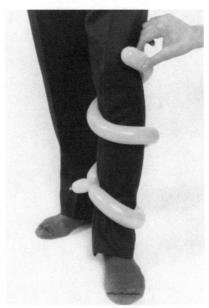
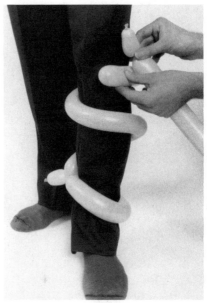

7. Begin wrapping the balloon like a candy-cane stripe, up the leg of the person who is wearing it.

8. Continue wrapping the balloon until you have run out of balloon.

9. Holding the wrapped balloon in place, pick up the other balloon, and make a 1-inch bubble below the knot of that balloon.

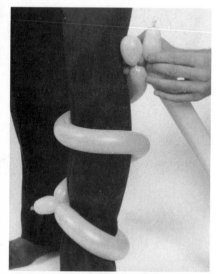

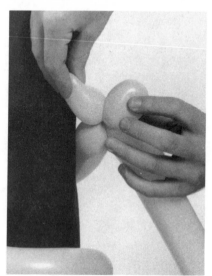

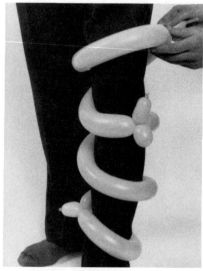

10. Make a 1-inch bubble on the tail end of the balloon that is wrapped around the person's leg.

11. Twist these two bubbles around each other a couple of times until they are locked together. You have just added a one-balloon extension to your balloon leg wrapping.

12. Continue wrapping the new balloon around the person's leg.

110

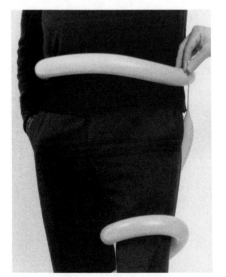

13. Leave enough balloon so that the second balloon can comfortably reach the Balloon Belt. You will attach the legging to the belt so that it will stay up.

14. Make a 1-inch bubble at the *tail* end of the second balloon.

15. Wrap this bubble around the Balloon Belt at the closest point where the legging reaches the belt.

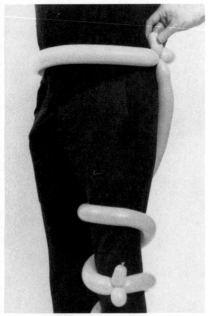

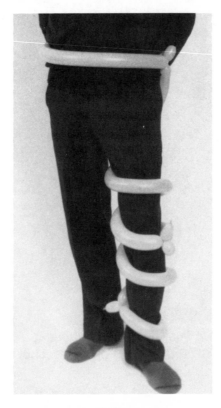

16. Wrap it around a couple of times. This will lock the legging in place and hold it up.

17. This is a completed Balloon Belt with Balloon Legging.

THE BALLOON SPACE SUIT

This is another great costume that builds off the belt.

1. Begin by making the Balloon Belt, the first item in this series.

2. Inflate and knot two more balloons, leaving 1-inch tails on the end of each.

3. Tie together the knots of each of the two balloons.

114

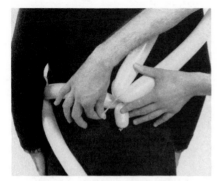

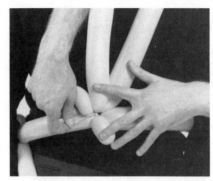

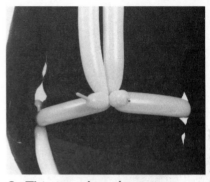

4. Take this double knot and wrap it around the body of the Balloon Belt, in the back of the belt.

5. Wrap it around twice so that it stays in place.

6. This attaches the two balloons to the Balloon Belt.

7. Pull the balloons over the shoulders of the person wearing them.

8. Pull the balloons down in front of the person, and tuck the two ends inside the belt, so that they are held in place.

9. This is the completed Balloon Space Suit. Try wearing it with the Balloon Legging, as shown in the photo.

ACCESSORIES

THE MASK

This is a fun accessory that adds a nice touch to any of the hats.

118

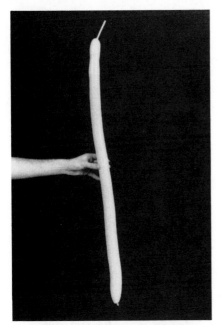

1. Inflate a balloon until you have a 3-inch tail on the end, and tie a knot.

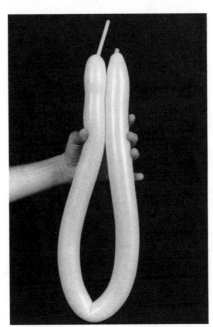

2. Fold the balloon in half.

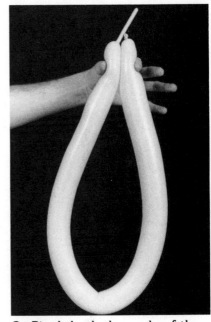

3. Pinch both the ends of the balloon with one hand, about one inch below the knot and the tail.

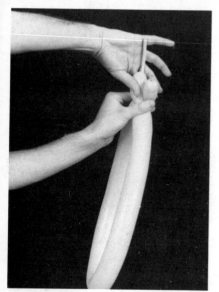

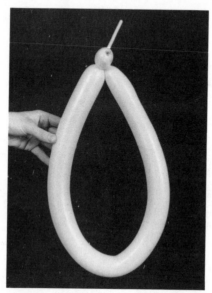

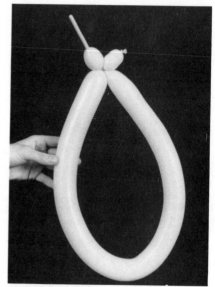

4. Twist the two bubbles that are formed around each other a couple of times.

5. This locks them together.

6. When you let go of the folded balloon, you will have a large balloon loop. Hold the loop so that the two bubbles are on top.

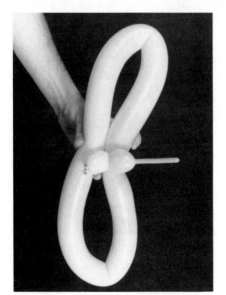

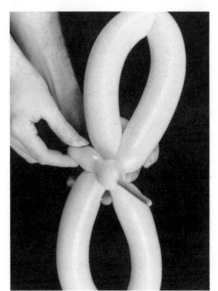

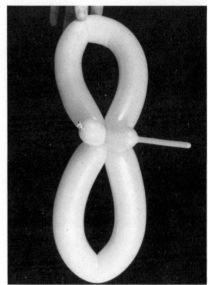

7. Now fold the loop in half again, with the two bubbles in the middle of the fold.

8. Take one of the bubbles and wrap it around the body of the balloon loop where the loop meets the bubbles. You need to wrap it around only once.

9. This is what your mask looks like so far. Position the two bubbles on top of each other.

10. Hold the mask up to your face, and spread the two large loops apart so that they can be placed on your nose, lightly pinching it.

11. Position it comfortably on your nose so that it will stay in place once you let go.

12. Now let go! This is the completed Mask.

THE BALLOON **SPRING**

This is a fantastic accessory to add to any of the balloon creations in this book and a great addition to any hats or costumes that you might invent. It can also be worn separately as a bracelet or anklet. You'll need a friend to help with this one.

1. Inflate a balloon all the way to the very end, but *don't* tie a knot.

2. Let all of the air out of the balloon.

3. Now repeat steps 1 and 2. Your balloon will look very stretched out.

will maintain a coiled shape much more easily. Hold the tail of the balloon between your thumb and the base of your index finger, on the inside of your hand. Let the rest of the balloon dangle down toward the floor.

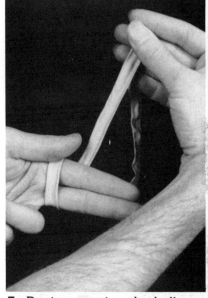

4. By inflating and deflating the balloon twice, you've stretched the balloon so it

5. Begin wrapping the balloon around your index finger *and* middle finger, in a coiled fashion. Wrap it first under your middle finger . . .

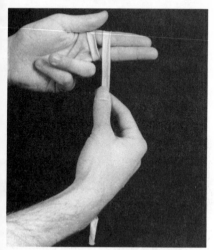

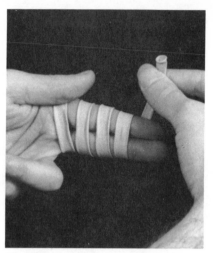

6. and then over your index finger.

7. Continue this motion until the balloon is almost entirely wrapped around your two fingers. Leave a little length of the balloon neck to inflate with the pump. Hold on!

8. Have your friend put the nozzle of the pump into the neck of the balloon, and begin inflating it.

126

9. As the balloon begins to inflate around your fingers, let the inflated part slowly slide off your fingers so that you have room for the rest of the balloon to inflate.

10. Inflate the balloon all the way to the end, still gradually letting the inflated part slide off your fingers. When the balloon is totally inflated, take the whole balloon off your fingers, and tie a knot.

11. Adjust the balloon coil if necessary. Sometimes it helps to recoil the balloon once it is inflated. This helps to tighten the coil.

12. This is the completed
Balloon Spring. It also
looks a great deal like a
balloon snake.

THE SWORD AND THE WAND

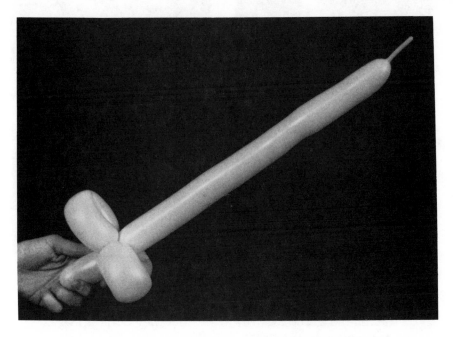

This is a dashing accessory to add to any balloon hat or costume. It may be carried in your hand or tucked inside your Balloon Belt.

 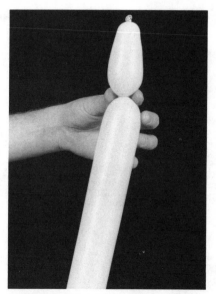 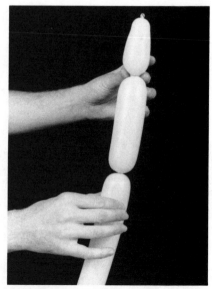

1. Inflate a balloon until you have a 3-inch tail on the end, and tie a knot.

2. Make a 2-inch bubble at the knot end of the balloon, and hold onto it. This will be the handle of the sword and the jewels on the tip of the wand.

3. Beneath that 2-inch bubble, make a 5-inch bubble and hold onto both bubbles so that they don't untwist.

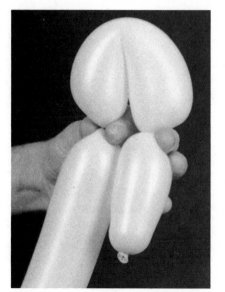 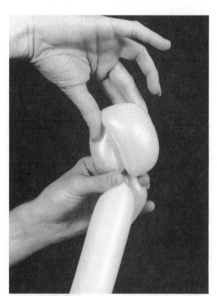 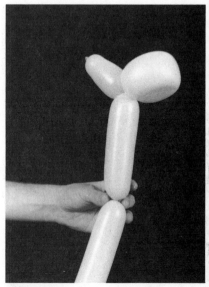

4. Fold the 5-inch bubble in half, so that its ends meet.

5. Twist the 5-inch bubble around on its ends a couple of times, until it is locked into place.

6. Make another 5-inch bubble, and hold onto it so that it doesn't untwist.

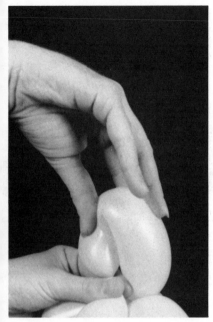

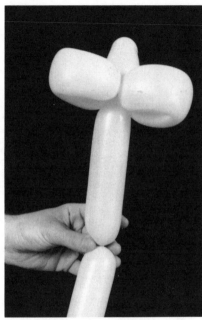

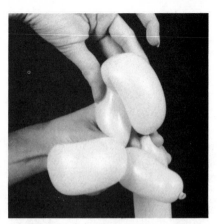

9. Fold this third 5-inch bubble in half so that its ends meet, and twist it around on its ends until it locks into place.

All three of the 5-inch bubbles will form the protective shield of the sword and the decorative top of the wand.

7. Fold this 5-inch bubble in half, and twist it around on its ends a couple of times, until it is locked into place.

8. Make another 5-inch bubble, and hold onto it.

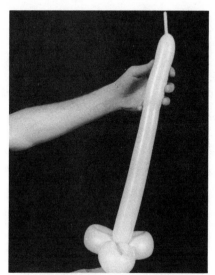

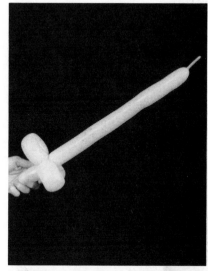

10. Position these three, folded 5-inch bubbles so that they are perpendicular to the handle (or top) and shaft of the sword (or wand).

11. Adjust the shaft of the sword/wand so that it is straight. Do this by simply straightening it out with your hands. Bend it in any direction that it needs to go to become straight.

12. This is the completed Balloon Sword. Just hold it upside down and it's a magic wand!

INVENTING YOUR OWN BALLOON HATS AND ACCESSORIES

The possibilities for creating your own spectacular balloon hats and accessories are literally endless. Balloons can be manipulated in many, many different and fascinating ways. I have made balloon hats and full balloon costumes that used forty or fifty balloons. There is no limit to where your imagination can wander when you let yourself go.

To help fuel your fantasies, I've included some photos of larger balloon costumes and hats for which I let *my* imagination go a bit. These photos illustrate quite well the limitless possibilities of *Balloon Hats and Accessories*. You really can't make any mistakes. Anything that you come up with is bound to be interesting.

For a few more suggestions, try inventing: a necklace, a bikini, an umbrella, a purse, a sash, other kinds of masks, a backpack, a microphone, a bouquet of flowers, a bow and arrow, a lasso, a fishing rod, a stethoscope, a broom, spats, a cane, and many, many more wild and zany balloon creations! I wish you many years of balloon fun. Cheer!

135

MAIL-ORDER SOURCES

If you are unable to find balloons or pumps at your local novelty, joke, or magic shop, try one of these mail-order sources:

Balloon Animals
P.O. Box 711
Medford, MA 02155
Balloons: $10.00 per bag (144 balloons per bag).
Pumps: $4.00 each, postage and handling included.*

Balloonology
P.O. Box 301
Cambridge, MA 02238
Balloons: $10.00 per bag (144 balloons per bag).
Pumps: $4.00 each, postage and handling included.*

*Massachusetts residents add 5 percent sales tax (50¢ per bag, 20¢ per pump).

Balloon Supplies
300-M Skokie Boulevard
Northbrook, IL 60062
Balloons: $10.00 per bag (144 balloons per bag).
Pumps: $4.00 each, postage and handling included.

Illinois residents add 7 percent sales t   ¢ per bag, 28¢ per pump)

For all   e
United $3.00
(U.S.) p